FRICTION

Wheels and Brakes

by Sally Hewitt

Aladdin/Watts
London • Sydney

FRICTION

Forces are pushes and pulls that make things change shape, move, speed up or slow down.

Friction is **force** that stops things moving or slows them down.

Dragging a tree

When you slide down a slope, friction slows you down.

When you drag something, it rubs against the ground. **Friction** slows the object down and stops it moving.

Note to Parents and Teachers

The READING ABOUT: STARTERS series introduces key science vocabulary and concepts to young children while encouraging them to discover and understand the world around them. The series works as a set of graded readers in three levels.

LEVEL 3: READ ALONE follows guidelines set out in the National Curriculum for Year 3 in schools. These books can be read alone or as part of guided or group reading. Each book has three sections:

• Information pages that introduce key concepts. Key words appear in bold for easy recognition on pages where the related science concepts are explained.
• A lively story that recalls this vocabulary and encourages children to use these words when they talk and write.
• A quiz asks children to look back and recall what they have read.

WHEELS AND BRAKES looks at FRICTION. Below are some answers and activities related to the questions on the information spreads that parents, carers and teachers can use to discuss and develop further ideas and concepts:

p. 6 *Which surfaces make the toy car slow down quickly?* When a toy car rolls on rough or bumpy surfaces such as a carpet there is more friction so it slows down quicker than on a smooth, flat surface such as a wooden floor or tiles.

p. 9 *What other objects need a smooth surface to help them work?* Anything that slides needs to be smooth, such as skis, snowboards and a computer mouse. Boats and planes also need a smooth shape to help them travel quickly through the water or air.

p. 11 *Is it easier to push the objects now?* Yes, it is easier to push the objects across the tray once it has been oiled. That's why cooks put oil on the bottom of a cake tin to help them remove the cake easily. Ask children to think of other objects that work better when they are oiled, e.g. squeaky door hinges, skateboard wheels, car engines.

p. 15 *How would you use the pads on the back of a rollerblade to slow down?* If you push your heel back the pads rub against the ground and friction slows you down. If you press harder the friction will make you stop. On a scooter you can also slow down by putting your foot on the ground.

p. 19 *Why would a bigger plate take longer to fall?* The bigger an object is, the more air resistance it creates. This friction with the air slows it down as it falls. That's why heavy objects need bigger parachutes than light ones.

p. 21 *Can you say how friction will slow a fishing boat down as it moves through the water?* Its rough sides and wide shape both create lots of water resistance, slowing it down.

ADVISORY TEAM

Educational Consultant
Andrea Bright – Science Co-ordinator, Trafalgar Junior School, Twickenham

Literacy Consultant
Jackie Holderness – former Senior Lecturer in Primary Education, Westminster Institute, Oxford Brookes University

Series Consultants
Anne Fussell – Early Years Teacher and University Tutor, Westminster Institute, Oxford Brookes University

David Fussell – C.Chem., FRSC

CONTENTS

© Aladdin Books Ltd 2007

Designed and produced by
Aladdin Books Ltd
2/3 Fitzroy Mews
London W1T 6DF

First published in 2007
in Great Britain
by Franklin Watts
338 Euston Road
London NW1 3BH

Franklin Watts Australia
Level 17/207 Kent Street
Sydney NSW 2000

Franklin Watts is a division of
Hachette Children's Books.

ISBN 978 0 7496 6872 3 (H'bk)
ISBN 978 0 7496 7594 3 (P'bk)

A catalogue record for this
book is available from the
British Library.

Dewey Classification:
531'.1134

Printed in Malaysia
All rights reserved

Editor: Jim Pipe

Thanks to:
The pupils of Trafalgar
Infants School, Twickenham, for
appearing as models in this book.

Photocredits:
*l-left, r-right, b-bottom, t-top,
c-centre, m-middle*
Cover tl & b, 2tl & bl, 3, 5tl &
br, 7 both, 8b, 10, 11tr, 12b,
15m, 22m, 23b, 31tr —
istockphoto.com. Cover tc, 6bl,
11br, 13tr, 14b, 16m, 18tr, 22bl,
24-26 all, 27tr & br, 28-29 all,
30, 31ml & mr — Marc
Arundale / Select Pictures. Cover
tr, 2ml, 6t, 9m, 17br, 18m, 20
both, 27ml, 31bl & br —
Corbis. 4tr, 5tr & bl, 15br, 16bl,
17t, 18mr, 21t & mr, 31bcl &
bcr — Photodisc. 4b — John
Deere. 8t — Courtesy Neoteric
Hovercraft Inc. 9br, 18br —
Digital Vision. 11ml — Corel.
13br — Deirdre Farrell. 14t —
Jim Pipe. 21br — Stockbyte.

When one surface rubs against another surface, **friction** is at work.
Here are some types of **friction**:

Wheels and road
When a car moves along, its tyres and the road rub together.

Boat and water
As a boat moves, water rubs against the sides and slows it down.

Ice skates and ice
Shiny skates and slippery ice rub together when a skater moves on ice.

Aeroplane and air
When an aeroplane flies, its body and the air rub together.

ROUGH SURFACES

When **rough surfaces** rub together they make more friction than when smooth surfaces rub together.

Motorbike

Wheels roll easily on a smooth surface, but when a motorbike rides over **rough**, bumpy ground it slows down.

Feel the floor surfaces in your house. Which ones feel rough?

Push a toy car over the different surfaces.
Which surfaces make the car slow down quickly?

When two **rough surfaces** rub against each other, friction makes them wear each other away.

Sandpaper is **rough**. A carpenter rubs sandpaper over **rough** wood to give it a smooth surface. The sandpaper gets worn away too.

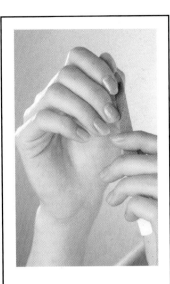

A rough nail file smoothes nails into a new shape.

Using sandpaper

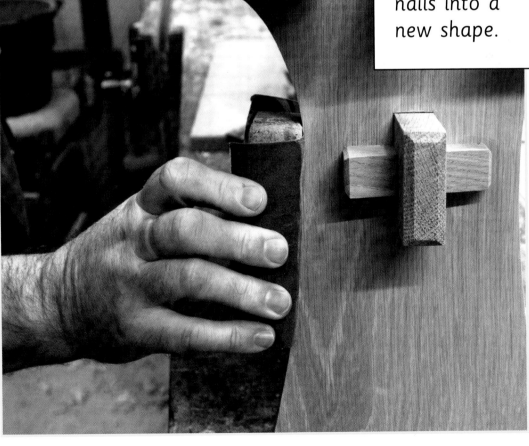

SMOOTH SURFACES

When **smooth surfaces** rub together, they make less friction than rough surfaces.

A bumpy track slows a car down. A car can go faster along a **smooth** road.

Smooth road

Air is smoother than water. A hovercraft speeds along on a cushion of air.

Floors made of marble or stone are polished to make them **smooth** and shiny. Be careful not to slip if the soles of your shoes are **smooth** and shiny too!

Even **smooth surfaces** such as a snowboard and snow make some friction when they rub together.

Snowboard

An iron has a smooth surface to help it slide over clothes.

What other objects need a smooth surface to help them work?

HIGH AND LOW FRICTION

Friction is a force we use every day.
There is **high friction** between
rough surfaces rubbing together.

Off-road car

Off-road cars have tyres with a deep tread.
There is **high friction** between the
rough tyres and the rough ground which
gives the tyres a good grip.

There is **low friction** between smooth surfaces rubbing together.

A playground slide is smooth and shiny. Smooth clothes rubbing against the slide make **low friction** so you can whizz down quickly.

A goalkeeper's gloves have a rough surface. This surface helps the goalkeeper grip the ball.

Slide

Oil helps to make low friction. We spray oil onto bicycle parts to help them move easily.

Push some objects across a tray. Then cover the tray with cooking oil. Is it easier to push the objects now?

ROLLING

Rolling makes less friction than dragging. Wheels make pulling things along much easier.

Before wheels were invented, people dragged heavy things along the ground. Friction made it very hard work!

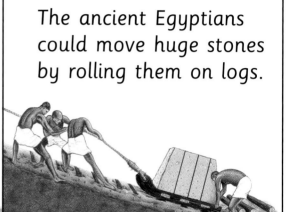

The ancient Egyptians could move huge stones by rolling them on logs.

These two children can move a big snowball by **rolling** it along the ground!

Rolling a snowball

Push a book along a table. It doesn't go fast because of friction.

Now roll the book along over some pencils. It is easier to push because rolling makes less friction.

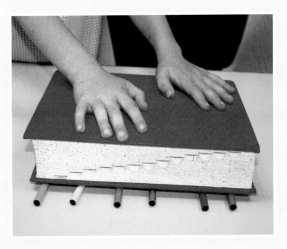

Wheels make less friction because only a bit of them touches the ground as they **roll**.

We push big loads along on wheels. Heavy shopping is easy to push in a trolley.

A wheelbarrow carrying a heavy load **rolls** along on one wheel.

Wheelbarrow

BRAKES

The **brakes** on a bicycle work because of friction.

When you squeeze the **brakes** on your handlebars, **brake** pads push against the wheels.

If you squeeze lightly, the **brake** pads only push lightly against the wheels and you slow down.

If you squeeze hard, the **brake** pads push hard against the wheels and you stop.

A toboggan has a smooth bottom that slips easily over snow. But it doesn't have **brakes!**

Dragging your feet in the snow makes friction. You use your feet instead of **brakes** to slow and stop the toboggan.

Toboggan

Rollerblades don't have brakes. They have pads on the front or back instead.

How would you use the pads to slow down? How would you use them to stop?

AIR RESISTANCE

Hold out your arms and run fast.
Can you feel **air** pushing against
you and slowing you down?

A force called **air resistance** slows down
anything that moves through the air.

Try throwing a beach ball.

It doesn't go far because
air resistance slows it
down very quickly.

Beach ball

A smooth, pointed shape helps an aeroplane fly faster. Its pointed shape helps it to move easily through **air**.

Smooth sides make low friction when **air** rubs against it.

Run along holding a big piece of card in front of you. Can you feel air pushing against it?

Now run holding the card with the edge facing forward. Why is it easier to run like this?

When an aeroplane comes in to land, flaps on the wings lift up. The flaps slow the plane down.

PARACHUTES

The shape of an object can slow it down as it falls through the air.

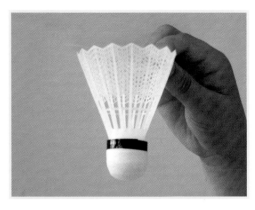

A tennis ball falls faster than a shuttlecock. Air is trapped by the shuttlecock feathers and slows it down.

A piece of paper floats down slowly when you drop it. Will it fall faster if you crumple it into a ball?

Tennis ball

Dandelion seeds have a shape that slows them down when they fall.

Blow on a dandelion and see how far the seeds float!

18

The shape of a **parachute** helps people to fall slowly through the air and have a safe landing.

Air gets trapped under the **parachute** as it falls and slows it down. The bigger the **parachute**, the more air gets trapped under it.

Parachute

Make a parachute by taping four equal lengths of string to a paper plate. Then attach the ends of the string to a plastic toy. Drop the parachute. Why would a bigger plate take longer to fall?

WATER RESISTANCE

It's hard work running through water! The water rubs against you and slows you down.

Friction called **water resistance** slows down anything that moves through the water.

When you swim, you make a long, pointed shape, like a fish. This shape helps a shark cut through water and swim fast.

Fish scales overlap, so water can slip over them easily.

Shark

Using a paddle

Water resistance can be a helpful force. When you push a paddle against the water, **water resistance** helps your paddle grip the water.

When you swim, **water resistance** helps you to push your body through the water.

This fishing boat has a wide shape and rough sides.

Can you say how friction will slow it down as it moves through the water?

MAKING HEAT

When two surfaces rub together, they make **heat.**
Friction lights a match. When a match
is struck on a rough surface it gets hot.

The **heat** makes chemicals in the end
of the match burst into flame.

Match

Friction makes
you warm.

You rub your hands
together to warm
them up on a cold day.

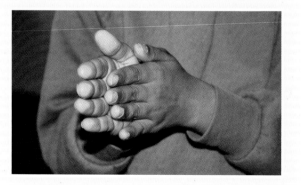

People have used friction to make fire for thousands of years.

They knocked flint stones together or rubbed sticks together to make a fire.

When cars have to brake suddenly, they sometimes skid. The tyres rub so hard against the road that friction **heats** them up.
You can smell burning rubber!

Skidding car

THE BIKE RIDE

Look out for ideas about friction.

"Can we go on a bike ride, Mum?" asked Georgia.

"It will be our first bike ride of the year," said Mum. "Let's check the bikes."

"Tyres first," said Jude. "They all need pumping up," said Mum, getting to work.

"Why have the tyres got patterns?" asked Jude. "They feel rough."

"It's for extra friction, so they grip the ground," said Mum.

"The soles of our shoes have got patterns too," said Jude.

"For extra friction!" said Georgia.

Jude tried out his bike. It was hard to make the pedals go around!

"The chain is rusty! I'll give it some oil," said Mum.

"Is that for more friction too?" asked Georgia.

"No," said Mum. "We want less friction. Oil makes the chain slippery so it moves over the cogs easily." "It's much easier to pedal now!" said Jude.

"Do the brakes need oiling?" asked Jude.

"No," said Mum. Brakes must grip the wheels. Oil would make them slippery. They wouldn't work."

"Tyres pumped.
Chains oiled.
Brakes checked.
Drinks packed.
Helmets on.
We're off!"
said Mum.

"Have we forgotten something?" said Georgia.
"I don't think so," said Mum.

They cycled through the park.
"It's easy riding along
the path," said Jude.

"The path is smooth,"
said Mum.

"For less friction!"
grinned Georgia.

They reached the river and cycled along the
towpath. "It's hard riding along here!" said Jude.
"The towpath is rough," said Mum.
"More friction," said Jude.

They cycled for half an hour along the towpath.

"I need a rest," said Jude. He braked too hard, skidded and nearly fell off his bike.

"Too much friction!" said Georgia. "You'll wear your tyres out!"

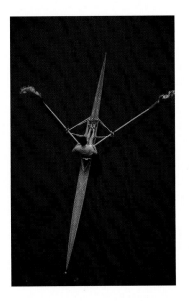

They had a drink and watched a rower speeding along in his boat.

"He's going faster than we did!" said Jude.

"It's a racing boat," said Georgia.

"It's long and pointed for cutting through the water."

"Like a shark!" said Jude pointing his arms and pretending to swim.

They set off again.

"Oh no! I've got a puncture!" said Mum.

"That's it! That's what we've forgotten. The puncture kit!" said Georgia.

"I can't ride my bike with a flat tyre," said Mum. "It's a long way. I'll have to push it home."

"Why can't you ride it?" asked Jude. "It still works."

"Because it would damage the tyre and the wheel," said Mum.

"Too much friction," said Georgia sadly.

"Don't worry, Mum, we'll ride slowly and keep you company," said Jude.

A kind cyclist stopped
and asked, "Can I help?"
They showed her the puncture.

Luckily the cyclist had a puncture
kit and soon mended Mum's tyre.
"Thanks!" they all said
and waved goodbye.

"I'm a bit cold now," said Georgia.

"Rub your hands together,
that will warm you up,"
said Mum.

"Why?" said Georgia.

"Because rubbing makes
friction and friction
makes heat and heat
warms you up!"
said Mum.

Georgia rubbed her hands.
"It really works!" she said.

When they got home, Dad was cooking pancakes for tea. Dad tossed a pancake and caught it perfectly.

"The oil in the pan makes it slippery," said Jude.
"The oil makes less friction."
"That's very clever, Jude!" said Dad.
"How do you know that?"

"I'll tell you after I've eaten my pancakes," said Jude.
Everyone laughed!

WRITE YOUR OWN STORY about friction. It could be about a journey. Make a list of things you do where friction is at work.
Are you using high or low friction?

Low friction	High friction
Opening a drawer	Using an eraser
Skating on ice	Cleaning dirt off your shoes
Skating on rollerblades	Rubbing your hands together
Sliding down a slide	Your bicycle tyres grip the road

QUIZ

Which make more **friction** when they rub together, **rough** or **smooth surfaces**?

Answer on page 6-7

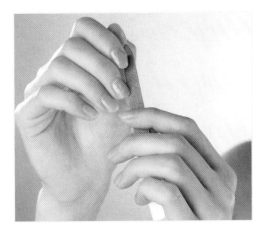

Does oil help to make more or less **friction**?

Answer on page 11

What does **friction** do when you rub your hands together?

Answer on page 22

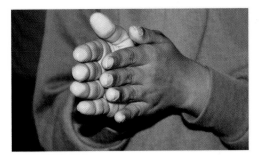

What surfaces are rubbing together in these pictures?

Answers on page 4, 5, 6, 9

INDEX